UNNOTICED NECESSITIES

PALAK OZA

"To my dear reader, who bears the burden of my thoughts."

Contents

Contents

Contents

Preface

The journey of writing this book started five years ago, sitting in the passageway of my house. Over these years, I have realised poetry is one of my closest friend, a listener, a mentor, and a source of joy. Most of the poems in this book spring mainly from observations, which go unnoticed. This is my attempt to capture those moments that seem to overwhelm me, and to discover myself as I reflect upon them.

Poems are not confined to feelings or logic alone and captivate the essence of everything. The beauty of poetry lies in the ways it can be written and the ways it can be read.

On that note, I invite you to take a deep dive into my sea of thoughts and perhaps there might be a wave in my sea that resonates with you too!

Happy Reading!

1. REFLECTIONS

"It's the smile of a heart,
peace to a restless mind,
it's music to the ears
and freedom of the soul."

-what poetry is to me.

2. Perhaps

"*If only words could carry*
the weight of what we felt,
perhaps,
we could fly."

3. What If

Lately,
my poems,
have been thrown out of whack.

Perhaps,
my words and emotions won't rhyme.
I won't be able to feel the sun,
or make the wandering winds run.

The words I never wrote,
form a lump in my throat.

And maybe the ink won't spill-
all of my secrets.
maybe the world won't-
hear my story.

But what chills me down,
to my very bones
is-
What if I can't remember
how it feels like to write?

4. LOVE

"I've been through experiences,
analyzed moments,
but,
never had I come across a feeling
like this one,
folks call it love."

5. Air

I fell in love with you,
Like the swift intake of breath,
And I didn't even realise when-
You became my air.

6. Celebration

Perhaps the universe is a marriage
where Saturn holds the ring,
where distant stars are dancing
and the meteors all sing.

Mother Earth is the bride
dressed up in blue and green,
and dear Moon is cheering by,
knowing she'll make a good queen.

Sun spreads it's blessings
the music of heaven in play,
as Earth walks down the orbit aisle
the planets all seem to sway.

The wind whispers this story
in the silence of the night,
just so the Earth can remember
it's love at daylight.

7. You

You are the warming sun to my heart's coldness.
You are the wave of emotions in my river of thoughts.
my heart sways to the tune of happiness in your presence,
my soul longs for your company,
my hands lifeless without your touch.

Every night when the magnificent moon peeps
through its veil of clouds,
and when the sky looks embedded with diamonds,
I am reminded of you.

Every time that I gaze into your eyes,
I drown,
for they are so deep with love.
Every time that a rose blooms,
it's flushed with colour,
blushing on seeing your beauty.

When your lips gently break into a smile,
it gives me the soothing feeling of existence.
Your kiss quenches my thirst
for eternal love.

Like the crystal dew drops of the mountain,
and the soft white snow,
you bring freshness to my life.

• 8 •

When you blink your eyes,
I think of the lapping water at sea.

When you hold my hand,
I melt-
like the dusky sky melts into the sea.
Then so gracefully,
like the withering away of rustic leaves in autumn,
my problems fade.

You are the sparkle in my eyes,
you are the poetry to my life,
you are my dawning inspiration,
you are the nature's beauty,
you are the smile of my face,
you are the love which I wish to bask in forever.

8. Fathom

I tried to fathom love,
to understand why the stars melted to rain,
why the sun kneeled every day in its honour,
why the seas danced to its tune,

And then it hit me-
perhaps it wasn't a feeling meant to be fathomed,
only to be felt,
and when I did,
I found my answer.

9. When I Say I Love You

When I say I love you,
I want to stir our memories in my morning cereal,
I want to soak in the sun and melt in pure ecstasy,
I want the birds chirping our stories to the world,
I want the sea to wash away our pain,
I want the stars to dance at our sight,

When I say I love you,
above all-
I want us to be together.

10. Fate

Dear lord , she prayed,
you can take everything away,
but promise me,
he'll be here to stay.
He did.
Her prayers lasted.
But she in her deathbed lay-
fate carried her away.

11. Blooming

• 12 •

When the grieving sky cries in love for Mother Earth,
Flowers bloom to remind him of his beauty.
When obstacles lie in destiny's path,
Love blooms to remind us of our strength.

12. Daze

Why is it?
humanly impossible.
to describe,
what I feel about you.
so simple a feeling, it's complicated to put to words.
-*The dictionary fell short*

13. Sugar

Perhaps your heart is made of sugar,
pure and transparent as it's crystals.
and when-
the walls are broken,
you spread your sweetness,
dissolving your love,
in my morning coffee.

14. Past, Present, Future

• 15 •

Your eyes hide my future.
your embrace shapes my past.
the curve of your smile,
oh darling,
rules my present.

15. Honey

Whoever says
'truth is bitter',
is wrong.
you're my truth and
you're like honey to my soul.

16. A Moment

I long for a moment
in the darkness of the night

no moon, no stars.

only you,
me,
the flickering fire,

and an infinite gaze.

17. Divine Love

It is so foretold-
when entering the souls garden,
the red roses seem to bloom-
blushing and flushed,
on seeing the beauty-
of divine love.

18. Warmth

You made my heart burn,
like the splendid sun.
you made me
the star of your galaxy.
made your world revolve around me.
I promise I'll keep you warm.
I will keep you warm.

19. Annotations

• 20 •

After my life's book is written,
I'll sit and highlight
the moments
that I spent with you.

20. MEMORIES

• 21 •

Pretty hearts are a world of experiences

21. Hidden Beauty

All those painful memories,
like pieces of shattered glass-
you join those broken bits,
and let them reflect your being,
as though the pain defines you.

So I gift you a mirror,
polished with your goodness,
just so you can see,
your long hidden beauty.

22. Essence

The pillow still reeks of coconut oil
and the juice box still half open
you've turned off the internet again
that's why the video paused
I know you've hidden the medicines
under the mattress
I know your legs hurt
but it's just the cold I promise
It's another forwarded "Good Morning" message
I'll translate it for you
We'll have dinner at eight sharp
I won't be late.
it's a little silent today
didn't hear you pray
I didn't hear you bang the door shut
or the squeak of your blue shoes
The crossword puzzle remains unsolved
the calendar page unturned
why am I mourning
the rising of today's sun?
-in loving memory of dadi

23. Ode To My Artist

I still remember-
you painted old bottles
for a school project.
who knew then
you'd become an artist?

Today,
you caress hearts with the stroke of your brush,
and emotions-
drip from your painted canvas,
smudged smiles,
tainted pain.

The pencil drawings-
stain your hands,
with love and charcoal,
intricately capturing-
the shine in your eyes.

Casually you go on,
without doing a thing-
but melting the whole universe,
into a white sheet.

24. Tides of Time

I walk by,
Watching the tides of time.
They crawl up to the shore,
As I watch-
Treasured memories,
Sinking in the sand.

I bottle up my moments,
And throw them in the sea.
Wishing someday perhaps,
They'll come floating back to me.

25. PAIN

I wanted to wash away my pain.
I jumped into the sea,
And as I was engulfed by the blue,
I realised how difficult it was to hold on.
To breath, to experience, to pain.

26. Teardrops

• 27 •

You wonder why I cry-
when the stars reside in my eyes.
But darling,
the ocean treasures teardrops of
the weeping skies.

27. I Know

I could see the pain,
in the flutter of your eyelashes.
I know you walked
straight into the shower
to wash your thoughts clean
Did you stare-
into the eyes of oblivion
till the darkness
made you cry?

I know
your bones
curled up under your skin
afraid.
but whatever was bodily pain
compared
to the burning of the heart?

28. Hide and Seek

The bags under your eyes
are heavy-
from all the words
you've not said.
the wave of thoughts,
have creased your forehead.
The game of Hide-and-Seek is still on,
I seek your smile.
I will not give up.

29. Gather

Perhaps we should have a label
just for our hearts,
"Fragile,
Handle with care."

It's a tedious task to collect the parts,
put them back together.
Acceptance
they say,
is a durable glue.

30. Essential

• 31 •

I went shopping today.
the store brimming-
lots to stuff into my bags.
tetra packs of sadness,
a can full of pride-
that I could swallow.
easy to cook dreams,
and cookies of joy.

But today,
I decided
I would only get what I needed.
so I filled my air bags with breath
and left.

31. I Wish

I wish you could see
the strength that hides behind your burning red eyes.
the compassion and forgiveness that so gracefully touches
your soul.

I wish you could see
the ocean of calmness that runs through your veins.
the river of thoughts that are pleading you to let go.

I wish you could see
how cutely your cheeks swell up every time you're upset.
how the momentary sadness veils a beautiful smile.

I wish you could see
that even through the darkest of nights you're not alone.
that everything that happens, happens for a reason.

32. Ceasefire

I'm at war with my mind.
I've tried -
to concentrate.
Distraction always breaks it free.

I seek shelter,
from bombing thoughts.
Memories are ablaze,
burnt to ashes.
lost-
perhaps forever.
judgement smogged,
the weather is rather grey.

Words are knights,
they fight for my sanity.
the pen a mighty sword.
I'm building an army,
recruiting-
from a tub of chocolate ice cream.

Don't pull the trigger just yet,
I tell my mind.

I'm still counting my blessings.

Truce?

33. Let Go

• 35 •

When my first dandelion bloomed,
I was convinced
the sun was jealous,
of the bright yellow flower.

It then grew
to a mystical white.
so fragile,
a gentle breeze-
could steal away its charm.

One evening,
the wind did its job.
like a group of swans,
the seeds took wing.
only one remained
clinging on.

Let go
I whispered.
let go.
sometimes,
it's a beautiful thing to do.

the spring,
awaits your birth.

My voice-
floating in the air,
My words,
Echoing in the wind,
As though they were-
tracing their way back to me.
Let go my love,
let go.

34. Magic

I wish magic existed,

With the swish of the wand,
I'd make your worries vanish.

I could show you,
how the death saw too
wouldn't be able to cut
through your heart.

What if I made you
levitate?
showing you-
that rock bottom was
perhaps necessary?

Or maybe,
I'd pull out the rabbit,
from the hat,
and you could follow him
into a wonderland.

Ultimately,

I'd lay down
a pile of cards
and wish-
the one you were holding,
was hearts.

35. Beauty

She looked so thin and weak,
with spots all over her cheek.
Her brows were unevenly thick,
The bagged eyes made her look sick.
her eyes were a dark, muddy brown,
while she wished them to be sea blue, so,
in them the world could drown.

Her hair was straight and greasy,
Her voice anxious and uneasy.
Her nose was fat and long,
everything with her seemed so wrong.

She gazed and gazed until she saw,
the beauty masked behind each flaw.
The freckles resembled stars of the night sky,
The hearts beauty none could deny.
The deep brown of her eyes was the humbleness of the earth.
No, the lean body didn't determine her worth.
Nobody cared about the shape of her nose,
because, in the end it's only her kindness that glows.
So yes you're beautiful, in your very own way,
and no opinion of the world, can steal your beauty away.

36. The Warrior

She had been scarred, but with pride,
as anger gushed through her veins ,
She had nothing to hide.
She was graceful, yet a fierce fire in her eyes.
She had risen from the ashes, of hatred, anger, and despise,
her mind was prepared , her heart atrocious.
And yet her soul was ambiguous.
Her kindness had faded and her love was masked.
For now in self joy and glory she basked.

Words were her unbroken swords and vibes her shield,
her armour, once a shining silver was,
now drenched in blood,
lost at field.
A burning heart groaned with despair,
drunken in melancholy of which she was unaware.

Slowly oh slowly she fell in regret,
her pain only worsened,
and her love slipped in the hands of debt.
The world seemed empty and so felt her heart,
what had she done?
Her mind was swollen and her soul ripped apart.

The chain of negative and pain is endless,

too heavy to be broken.

she had left the voices in her head unheard, unspoken.

the world is filled with gloom,

let's give up on our revenges and let the joy bloom.

We deserve better, so did she,

Conquer your regrets and embrace the Glee.

Only then will your soul be truly free.

37. Gem Of A Person

• 42 •

Blood gushes through her veins,
like a ferocious river.
Her hair cascading down,
like a brown waterfall.
her eyelids flutter,
like butterflies-
of the hidden valley.
and her precious heart-
remains enclosed in her ribs,
like an oyster protects the pearl.

38. Lady Macbeth

She hid it deep in her heart,
guarded by love, for her counterpart.
Lady Macbeth knew it all,
but she was too scared to fall.
She fought her guilt day and night,
but as the summers passed by,
her guilt only gained more might.
She battled pain, all in vain.
but her compunction stabbed her again.
Neither her royal bed nor her designed clothes could give her
comfort,
her gloom however remained unhurt,
trust was a misdeed and loyalty a sin,
while hope gave her a nasty grin.
Depressed, unable to bear the load,
with dignity, to death she bowed.
She had won the battle, but inside she was heartbroken,
the shine of victory on her face but sorrow in her eyes
unspoken,
deed weighed more than laurels,
in greed she had crossed all her morals,
Death freed her of the chains of guilt.
But what had she gained? What had she built?

She lost all faith in one go,
She had no feelings of love or sorrow.
Finally, she realized that deed had returned,
and self-hatred is all she had earned.
Victory is priceless, but so is life,
happiness or sadness on what do you want to survive?
*Based on William Shakespeare's play The Tragedie of Macbeth.

39. She

She's an entanglement of beauty,
She's the whirl of Chaos in my mind and yet the peace of my heart.
She veils her charm in humbleness like the supple green bud that encloses the flower,
She isn't bound by the lucid imagination of poets,
she herself is poetry,
written,
by enchanted hearts.
She reflects her joy, her compassion,
as the glint of light falls on the broken pieces of her crystal heart.
She's rain,
she washes away my troubles as her voice gently trickles down with mingled concern.
And when she sits,
lost in her forest of thoughts,
her brown locks flutter in the air
She burns brightly like a flaming candle,
her eyes so subtle as though they enclose the mysteries of the world
in the darkness of the night, when the world sleeps,

her voice gently whispers to me and I drown into joyous
dreams.

her comforting words weave a blanket for my bleak and cold
days.

sometimes when she talks about her passions,

I wander and explore her heart only to be left in awe.

She sees through my emotions like sunlight penetrating
spider's web.

She's unfathomable and yet so simple!

Destiny finds us together

as she gracefully walks on the shore of my soul,

leaving her footsteps behind,

as she dives into the deepest portions of my heart.

40. DREAMS

• 47 •

"Follow your Dreams", chase them like the streak of light that tails a shooting star.

41. Cake

I've never really liked the icing,
(too sweet)
or the cherry on top.
I want to know,
the heart of the cake.
An edible sponge,
oozing emotions,
and flavour. (in the life of some)

I want to know,
the slightly crunchy crust,
the layers of sweet and dark,

I want to know,
if it will hold the candles.
After all,
the weight of wishes-
is more than just a blow.

42. Faded Dream

In her mind's garden,
a beautiful flower blooms-
cracking through the humble soil.
blooming then with age,
to a lush red.

One day,
she stops nurturing it,
watering it with hope.
It withers away-
a faded dream.

43. Hope

All my dreams that faded away,
like fallen leaves-
in my path,
even when trodden on,
rustled of hope.

44. Rise

She fell.

Dreams and aspirations-
crumbled and burnt to ashes .

The sky collected them.
Hope twinkled.
A new diamond adorned the sky that night.
-how stars are formed

45. Ruin

Embrace it.
Ruin is a blessing my love,

Why else do you presume-
Autumn exits?
To celebrate ruin,

with the confetti of falling leaves.

46. Weeping

• 53 •

If anyone is ever wondering,
how grief leads to growth,
watch, the overwhelmed sky,
cry its heart out.
Every tear,
slowly blooming,
into life.

47. UNIVERSE

•54•

I rest my head on dreams,
tucked in a blanket of memories,
gazing,
at the eyes of the universe as they blink.
The midnight wind is listening,
to the secrets that I store-
of all the wants,
that wash up on my shore.
I want to knit a dress
from the threads of moonlight.
Pluck Saturn –
and wear it on my ring.
I want to stand on a meteor
and surf-
through the stars as they sing.
I want to feel the sun,
burning in my heart,
and let the vaccum-
hide stories of the Big Bang.
I want to insert the galaxy,
in a gramophone,
and listen-
to the music of the Universe.*

*Written by Palak Oza in "Discovering The Secrets Of The Universe" an Anthology by Nistha Bajpai.

• 55 •

48. Waves Of The Cosmos

• 56 •

If only
I could set up a camp
on the moon
and go fishing
in the sea of stars.

49. Identity

Somewhere in an alternate universe
she rises with the moon,
living the life of a forgotten past.
Every repeated mistake is new,
every feeling, never felt before.
That first kiss.
That broken trust.
Renewed.
She's not afraid.
to fail,
to break.
Because she knows she will forget.
So she lives,
without caution, without fear.
And yet,
Jealous,
of the alternate universe.
Our universe.
Where we remember,
the definition of our name.

50. Light Of The Universe

Today,
I looked at the night sky-
And wondered,
why do stars bother to burn so bright?
Engulfing themselves in flames,
just to be a dot in the universe,
seen from afar?

But little does the star know,
it's guiding someone on a rough night,
it carries the dream of a little child,
that its slow dance gets us hooked,
and that cities long to see it's glow.
perhaps,
people are stars-
with burning hearts.
sometimes unnoticed,
but together,
lighting up
the universe.

51. Hidden Universe

• 59 •

The universe is a flowing river,
And the earth a sailing boat,
stars are dancing waves,
And the sun is our hope.
You're the light of galaxies,
All planets ash and blue,
You're the living beauty,
the universe hides in you.

52. Have You Ever

Have you just ever stopped to see,
this world's long hidden beauty?
How the seashells embedded in the golden of the sand,
ornament the bay.
How the rustic autumn leaves are whispering that change is
here to stay!

Have you ever stopped to see?
How the frail bud hold beauty in disguise,
or how the ocean treasures teardrops of the weeping sky,
how the gusts of heaven, sing a song as they blow,
how the soil in love embraces all the seeds that we sow.

Have you just ever stopped to see?
The glow of stars in the depths of night,
how the misty clouds are penetrated by the orange sunlight,
how the river flows along, like feelings of a loving heart,
how the frosty winter has come, only to depart.

Have you just ever stopped to see?
What mysteries, lingering shadows of the forests veil,
and how the rugged mountains all tell a beautiful tale,
how the soothing silence has a language of its own,

and how this momentary stillness is telling us we have grown.

• 61 •

53. Travel

The whistling winds are calling
to journey through the seas,
verdant valleys welcome
the glory of new born leaves.
Journey through the seas
explore the forests forlorn —
the glory of new born leaves
in the tainted bits of dawn.
Explore the forests forlorn
as verdant valleys welcome
the tainted bits of dawn.
The whistling winds are calling.

54. Dawn

The sky has a glory that no one can deny.
The sea has depth that can never run dry.
but dawn,
Oh dawn reminds me-
that they are the prettiest when they meet.

55. Rain

The land was left broken,

thirsty for love and comfort,

the sky wept tears of compassion,

that so gently kissed the earth.

Old wounds healed,

the dirt washed away.

Damp freshness in the air,

The dusky clouds a shield

from the fiery wrath of sun.

As though the sky was a painting,

an abstract purple with tainted bits of grey.

The paint slowly dripped from the canvas,

washing the trees and the blooming flowers.

From a lush green leaf,

hung a tiny raindrop,

a crystal pendant in mother Nature's necklace.

From the merging of these liquid diamonds,

was formed the mighty ocean.

I stood in the rain,

soaked in happiness,

every drop sang the melody of the universe,

every splash a renewed love,

like rain penetrates the soil and nurtures it,
joy seeped through the deepest portions of myself-
and I felt a warmth I couldn't fathom.

56. Glowing

We never look at the sun,
never at its peak,
only at dawn and dusk.
Perhaps people are similar,
we see them rise and fall,
and never really notice-
when they glow the most.

57. Hold on

The ocean is a piano,
the sun and moon both play.

To the music of heaven,
sea gulls seem to sway.

The wind whispers stories
of islands far away.

The sand holds onto my feet
pleading me to stay.

58. LIFE

• 68 •

We are all prisoners of our expectations and then, the reality sets us free.

59. Why

Why are our emotions masked behind these phoney smiles?
Why do we shape our entanglement in pretty lies?
What if our hearts feelings were so intense, so passionate, that they had to be kept caged in our ribs?
Why are our wants a bottomless pit?
Why are there no Happy endings to our satisfaction?

Why do we knock on every door, roam every street , in search of happiness when we know we will find it only in ourselves?
Why do we hold on to things as though they were a rope to our survival?
When we are well aware that happiness from things is more undependable than a child's mood.

Why are we so hungry for fame, for conditional love, that we deliberately let ourselves to slip into a human we were never meant to be?
Why is it that the world is so full of people and yet it feels so empty?
Why do we let our past drag us down and not let our future take wing?
Why does our joy reside in distant stars , when we ourselves are more unfathomable than the universe?

What is it that stops us? Who really are we?

Are we only a product of our errors or are we the pride of our experiences?

Why are we so lost in exploring the world, in pushing our way through, that we have forgotten to explore ourselves?

Why do we never question, are we too afraid or are we too ignorant?

60. Shadows

We all copy our idol,
their idea, their nature-
become someone we are not.
perhaps we're not really living,
just shadows gasping for breath.

61. Friendship

Blooming flowers that fragrance the air,
sunlight that warms up the tree's heart.
moon that never leaves earth's side,
and sea that dilutes all sadness of the sand.

Stars that always hang out together,
waves that dance together through pink and pain.
clouds that embrace the mountains,
and dew that loves Earth's morning face.

It makes me think we were born in friendship.
That we were moulded by it.

Perhaps, we were all friends once,
taught to love, share and care,
separated then by distance and time -
but still breathing the same air.

62. Treasured Moments

I've always thought of our lungs
to be a treasure box,
with every intake of breath,
a priceless moment,
added–
to the treasure.

Make every breath count,
I've been told.

63. Joy

The unnoticed smiles,
unseen destinations,
unheard stories,

The warm hug,
interlocked fingers,
gazing eyes,

The lousy Sundays,
coffee stains,
scent of books,

The sunlight on my face,
ripples in water,
wind in my hair,

Happiness.

64. Gratitude

• 75 •

To failure that haunts my evening showers,
To those medals polished with success,
To lost moments that leak from the tap of time,
To the sun that rises with hope,

To fear and to joy,
To nature's creation,
And to the life well lived,
Thank you.

65. Unfinished Book

Strength is a blooming flower,
Regret is the road not taken,
Comfort is a cup of cinnamon tea,
Vanity is a smiling mirror,
Hope is the dance of stars,
Dream is a fluttering butterfly,
Beauty is an unnoticed smile,
Care is the gently falling rain,
Anger is the piercing sun ray,
Imagination is the splash of colours,
Opinion is a concrete wall,
Life is an unfinished book.

UNNOTICED NECESSITIES

"I wish my poetry to you was-

like the reminiscing of a moment,

like the smell of fresh print,

like the gaps between your fingers,

like the very air we breathe.

An Unnoticed Necessity. *"*

Acknowledgements

Thank you,

to Mumma and Papa who always supported me.

Thank you,

to my family and friends who have always encouraged me.

And finally,

thank you,

dear reader, for your time.